Making Money
While Saving Money

The Expense Reduction Analysts
Franchise Opportunity Revealed

Dr. John P. Hayes

Paperback Publication Date: 2017
ISBN: 978-0-9975536-8-0
Publisher: BizComPress
Copyright, 2017, Expense Reduction Analysts and John P. Hayes, Ph.D.

First edition published 2017
BizComPress
A division of BizCom Associates
BizComPress.com
1400 Preston Rd #305, Plano, TX 75093

Read this Disclaimer

Please note: Neither this book, its author, or its publisher provide counsel or advice. This book and its contents are not intended for the purpose of buying a franchise. This book is a tool that might possibly be helpful in the process of evaluating a franchise business prior to investing in it. No one should invest in a franchise or any business based solely on the information in this book. Investing in a franchise is a serious matter that requires thorough investigation of the franchise opportunity, the franchisor, and related subjects. Franchising is not for everyone. The reader is advised to consult with a licensed professional for legal, financial and other professional services. The reader of this book assumes responsibility for the use of this information. The author and publisher assume no responsibility or liability whatsoever for the use or misuse of the information contained within this book.

Other Best-Selling Books by Dr. John P. Hayes

Visit: BooksByJohnHayes.com

Visit: *BooksByJohnHayes.com*

101 Questions to Ask Before You Invest in a Franchise

Take the Fear Out of Franchising

Buy "Hot" Franchises Without Getting Burned

12 Amazing Franchise Opportunities for 2015

**Franchising: The Inside Story
with John Kinch**

7 Dirty Little Secrets of Franchising: Protect Your Franchise Investment

How To Buy A Franchise: Collection Volume 1

Amazing Franchise Business Ideas

Praise for
Making Money While Saving Money
The Expense Reduction Analysts
Franchise Opportunity Revealed

"Becoming an expert in franchising is not the most important thing when learning about the opportunity with Expense Reduction Analysts. Leveraging another's expertise is. This book does just that. Not only does it provide phenomenal color to the black and white outline of what it is to be a part of ERA, it gives a great high-level view of franchising as a whole. This book allows immersion into the day to day (as well as the long term view) as a franchisee with ERA to the point where one can confidently move forward in their exploration."

- Brandy Reed, Business Consultant, FL

"*Making Money While Saving Money* provides a useful perspective on how a franchise business model works for a professional services business like Expense Reduction Analysts. Through the franchise model, a group of smart, motivated, experienced professionals work together to provide tangible savings benefits to clients that can be measured in dollars."

- Joe Brown, Business Consultant, WA

"ERA can work for a variety of people that come from many situations. In my case, I had previously been a partner in a CPA firm and a CEO of a mid-sized company. I had many contacts that allowed me to launch a business quickly by leveraging relationships developed in the first 26 years of my career. I was able utilize 26 years of problem solving for clients by bringing together teams of ERA subject matter experts to develop tremendous solutions that generated cash flow for their companies!"

– Jim Schmitt, Franchisee, Iowa

Making Money While Saving Money
The Expense Reduction Analysts
Franchise Opportunity Revealed

Contents

FOREWORD

IF YOU'RE IN THE BUSINESS of making money while showing clients how to save money, and you can do both whenever you wish and from wherever you desire, then you've got an amazing business.

Add to that the feeling that your business is making a huge difference for people and you've discovered almost everyone's dream business.

Except for you, it could be real!

It is real, in fact, for more than 650 consultants who own an Expense Reduction Analysts (ERA) franchise in more than 27 countries around the world. ERA's North American headquarters in Dallas, Texas, supports more than 150 franchisees.

ERA is rapidly expanding across the United States, and this book is an overview about ERA's franchise opportunity for individuals just like you who may want to start an ERA consulting practice.

If you're comfortable developing relationships with C-suite executives, and you enjoy working with teams who are part of the ERA network, then ERA is an opportunity to explore. This book will give you a deeper understanding of ERA's business model as well as insights from several franchisees.

ERA franchisees work primarily with CEOs and CFOs to help them discover cost savings in one or more of several dozen cost categories, such as telecommunications, healthcare, and office supplies, to name a few.

ERA franchisees can specialize in new business, manage ongoing client relationships, or focus on specializing in one or more cost categories to find cost savings for ERA's clients.

Both development and category specialists work together to deliver astonishing results. To date, ERA's global network has tackled more than 18,000 projects and found savings of nearly $1 billion!

About 5 years ago, Michael Nicholas was appointed president of the North American office, and he made system wide growth his first priority. Since that time, average franchisee income has doubled, average client size has doubled, and the number of projects per client has almost tripled.

Nicholas is fond of telling franchisees to focus on their "highest level of activity," meaning that they should concentrate on doing what they're best at doing, whether it's attracting new business or continuing to find cost savings for existing clients. When everyone is doing what he or she likes doing most, everyone wins.

Nicholas is doing what he does best. His franchise career spans more than 35 years, including 5 years as CEO of ERA Australia. He also worked within the McDonald's corporation for 27 years.

To help him sell franchises, Nicholas recruited Matt "Red" Boswell, Chief Growth Officer. For many years, Boswell has been helping people start their own businesses.

Boswell says he was attracted to ERA because it represents everything that he appreciates most about franchises: low or no inventory, franchisees can work from anywhere, and a service business with residual income.

By the time you finish reading this book, you may want to become part of ERA's growth. This franchise opportunity may be the perfect business for you.

– Dr. John P. Hayes

Expense Reduction Analysts

EXPENSE REDUCTION ANALYSTS: MAKING MONEY WHILE SAVING MONEY

WHAT DO A FORMER **PGA TOUR** EXECUTIVE, a tech company CFO, and a scientist with a Ph.D. all have in common? Despite vastly different career paths, their entrepreneurial spirit led them to the same place: an Expense Reduction Analysts (ERA) franchise.

They longed to be their own boss and preferred a tried-and-true franchise with ongoing support, a network of bright, cooperative franchisees, and a valued brand.

So what made them choose ERA?

Marylou Garcia, a former CFO, says she knew a good thing when she saw it, even though she wasn't really looking. Her sister was vetting possible franchises and asked Marylou to run the numbers. ERA caught her attention.

"I'm not your visionary that goes in and says, 'I'll make my own company (starting from scratch)' so franchising made sense," she says.

Tim Hawes, who once was a senior executive with the PGA TOUR, now has the flexibility to work when he wants … and even hit the links when he chooses.

"The lifestyle that (ERA) affords was important to me. It's entrepreneurial; it allows me to work from home and capitalize on the network of contacts that I had developed over the last 35 years," he says. "I was not looking to go back into a rigid corporate environment and that was important to me and significant with ERA."

That flexibility appealed the most to Becky Kalinowski, a scientist who one day dreamed of working for a major pharmaceutical company. But when her son was born 10 weeks early, everything changed. With ERA, being her own boss with a greater work/life balance was possible.

"Two kids and 7 years later, I'm a franchisee . . . I can be home with (my children) and still do scientific analysis – but now I work on financial analysis," she says.

Dreaming beyond corporate America

Kalinowski, Hawes and Garcia had bigger dreams beyond corporate America. They imagined working on their own in their own office. They imagined calling the shots and not being required to hire any employees because they were capable of doing the job quite well all by themselves. ERA offered them – and so many franchisees before them – a fresh start.

"Our brand image is a global consulting firm – that's the caliber of our franchisees – who come from a wide variety of backgrounds and have had enough of corporate politics and limitations," says ERA's Chief Executive Officer, Michael Nicholas. "ERA provides its franchisees a vehicle to have a fulfilling career *and* life."

Does this sound like the perfect business for you? Here's a closer look at what ERA does and its proven track record.

ERA works with clients to reduce costs and increase profits. The franchisees work with C-suite executives and build relationships with them throughout their journey. Market potential is extraordinary; companies are always looking for ways to save money and create more revenue.

A worldwide network of specialists

Look at these numbers:

ERA North America, headquartered in Dallas, Texas, is a globally recognized franchise with more than 650 consultants in more than 27 countries worldwide and growing daily.

While the majority of ERA franchisees are based outside of the United States – in England, Germany, Australia and elsewhere – more than 150 franchisees are supported by ERA's North American headquarters. Recently, ERA launched a campaign to rapidly increase franchise locations in the United States.

So who makes a great ERA franchisee? It is a people business. So, anyone who enjoys working with clients, suppliers, stakeholders and building relationships can make a great ERA franchisee.

"People think we're looking for analysts, but primarily we're looking for successful people who can speak comfortably to other C-suite executives and communicate effectively. They don't need in-depth accounting or analytical experience," says Nicholas.

He continues, "Over 95 percent of our cost saving projects are joint ventures between the franchisees who acquired the clients and the expense category specialist who finds the savings for the client. This allows our franchisees to focus on what they do best, either business development or category specialization.

At first, franchisee Marylou Garcia wasn't interested in being a business developer. But she got out of her comfort zone and started discussing the ERA solution with her peers. By doing so, she has more than doubled her income from her previous corporate role.

"When I talked to the ERA corporate office, I said, 'If this requires any bit of selling whatsoever, this is not for me. I don't sell. I'm on the finance side. Vendors come to me.' Those were my words, but business development is now one of the key roles I perform."

Once Garcia was able to figure out how to clear her biggest hurdle – getting past the CFO's gatekeeper – business started picking up. She was able to save her first client 30 percent of their costs for small package freight. Garcia's first monthly check was $6,000. She credits an ERA franchisee mentor with helping her land that first client and finding a successful return.

That ERA spirit of teamwork also helped Becky Kalinowski, who put her scientific background to good use as an expense category specialist, partnering with those needing her analytical skills.

"People are always impressed by the ERA entrepreneurial culture and the caring nature of the franchisees – they enjoy working with one another," says Nicholas.

Tim Hawes, who spent nine years at the PGA TOUR running their global products licensing business, says that internal support is one of many reasons he decided to become an ERA franchisee.

"I was very impressed with the quality of the internal team, very talented and dedicated, smart people in a well-structured, strong internal support system," he says. "I'm absolutely confident that when it comes to putting together superior teams for saving clients money while maintaining quality, we have the tools to do it."

A cooperative franchise network

ERA is a trusted global brand with the added value of a vast franchisee network. Franchisees certainly aren't solo businesses hanging out a shingle and going it alone. With ERA's proven system and extensive franchisee network, each franchisee can focus on his or her own area of expertise.

"The relationship between the franchisees is solid. There is a lot of communications between franchisees and you can call or email anyone – everyone welcomes questions," says Becky Kalinowski. "For example, if you've got a new project and you want to talk with other franchisees who have worked on similar projects, everyone is happy to help you succeed."

ERA gives franchisees opportunities to communicate with one another at area meetings throughout each year, as well as at an annual conference. Together, they discuss challenges and celebrate their successes. The gatherings also give the corporate support team a chance to further communicate and implement new corporate initiatives and professional development opportunities.

"These meetings give you, as a franchisee, the opportunity to network face to face with people from across the country and the globe," says Kalinowski.

Discover ERA

ERA also provides ongoing training, which sets the ground for a successful launch and continuing success.

Future franchisees go through the Franchise Discovery Process, a 10-step process that can take a minimum of three weeks and up to twelve weeks, depending on the pace of the franchise candidate.

After completing this process, franchisees attend a two-week training program in Dallas with

ERA corporate staff. Then the franchisee completes follow-up support training, which consists of ongoing calls, webinars, in-person trainings and more. In the final step, the franchisees are given advanced courses and internal certifications covering all aspects within an ERA franchise.

Tim Hawes, who became a franchisee in July 2016, was impressed with ERA's two-week foundation training.

"That's a very intensive two-week period where other franchisees from around the world are there and you learn everything about the business – administrative, sequencing, etc. It's a huge data consumption exercise over the course of a couple weeks and extraordinarily valuable," he says.

ERA franchisees enjoy two weeks of foundation training.

Coaching Franchisees

Coaching is also a big part of ERA training. Franchisees experience ongoing coaching in client acquisition, client management, and project analytics delivered by experienced franchisees throughout North America.

ERA's success can be partially credited to being a member of the International Franchise Association (IFA), which has helped the franchise in growth, development, and direction. ERA takes an active role in the IFA, the world's largest franchise association, and participates in their annual convention, political action committee, and educational seminars.

Other means of support for franchisees also include proven marketing tools, centralized billing and collection, and disbursement of cash flow to all parties.

"We provide centralized client billing and collections on behalf of franchisees," says Nicholas. "Let's say you have four clients and you get five to eight projects from those clients. We receive the payment from the clients for the projects and disburse it to the franchisees. This process saves franchisees a ton of time and hassle."

What do franchisees do?

So what does a typical ERA project look like?

"Each franchisee decides which vertical or verticals they want to pursue," says franchisee Becky Kalinowski. "ERA works in a variety of different markets including healthcare, manufacturing, professional services, education, etc."

Most clients feel confident that they've already done everything possible to keep costs down, but ERA franchisees advise them that it's worth another look. Consulting with them is a bit easier when the clients know they bear no financial risks. ERA only gets paid if there are savings to be gleaned from a project. And they split the savings 50/50 with the client for two years or more!

"The client's attitude is often, we have already found all the savings so 'Go for it,' and 'good luck' type of thing," says Kalinowski.

An ERA category-specialist-focused franchisee reviews a client's historical data of purchases for potential cost savings opportunities. We undertake a market analysis and we work with suppliers to obtain the lowest cost without sacrificing quality.

"Clients trust that we know the products well enough that we know how to get the exact product at a lower cost," explains Kalinowski.

Kalinowski recalls one of her now-favorite clients who was convinced that she couldn't uncover any additional cost savings for them. On the contrary, she was able to find a 17 percent savings and win the client over. She has earned their repeated business as they look for further ways to reduce costs.

For ERA clients, seeing is believing.

As an example, "If a client is spending $1 million, we may come back with $100,000 in savings. They never thought that was possible," Kalinowski continues, "but that is money they can put back into the business to expand and grow."

Who wouldn't want to save money while maintaining quality?

Typically, a client will have five to ten expense categories that need to be looked into for cost reduction. Clients have their own procurement team, but their staff can't be specialists in each field. They are procurement generalists. ERA includes specialists in more than 40 common expense categories! So if the client is spending $250,000 annually on office supplies, the ERA specialist, who knows that niche, will often know how to save 10 percent or more. Do that in five to 10 categories per client and a franchisee can build a lucrative business.

Franchisees share cost savings with clients
In the ERA model, the franchisee's fee is based on actual savings and the fee is shared 50/50

between franchisee and client over a 24-month timeframe.

For Tim Hawes, the appeal of running a franchise went beyond solid numbers and support. He was at a stage in his career where he wanted a dramatic change. ERA's unique product, quality people, solid business model, broad service platform and success fee structure were the main features that attracted him to the business.

Advantages of owning an ERA franchise

Franchisees tout the many personal advantages of owning an ERA franchise.

Flexibility and a family-friendly aspect of running an ERA franchise has been a perfect fit for Kalinowski.

"I realized time was a huge draw and selling point – I could get into the workforce and still be able to accommodate my family's schedule. I work from home," she says.

No expensive storefronts or inventory

No need for an expensive brick-and-mortar storefront with ERA. And in this service industry, inventory is nonexistent. That means upfront investment is much lower than other franchises. And with residual income coming in, franchisees can focus on long-term revenue.

"I'm personally expecting to earn a very comfortable living out of this business recognizing it's going to take 12 to 18 months before I see the income stream become significant," says Hawes. "I would expect to be within 3 years at least at the quarter-million-dollar-level of earnings if not significantly above. I didn't get into this for batting practice. I expect to be at the level of my corporate job, which was higher than $250,000 a year, and $500,000 a year earnings is not out of the realm of reasonableness."

The only possible challenge to starting a franchise is the ramp up of client payments. Franchisees will need an initial financial cushion as those first client billing payouts take a bit of time to roll in.

Hawes says he knew there would be lengthy lead-time, and he's fine with that.

"It takes time to get the business up and running and established, but then it's synergistic and builds on itself."

"I'm honest (with prospective franchisees) about first-year earnings," says Garcia. "If you have a college-bound kid and you can't support yourself through year one (of owning a franchise), this may not be right for you – unless you can draw on savings. If your goal is to get out of corporate life and have balance in your life, the ERA franchise puts control back in your hands."

The benefits far outweigh the negatives, says Kalinowski. "If you become a franchisee of ERA, and you join our network of franchisees, you are going to get an arsenal of very talented people to work with on projects," she explains.

Garcia points to the flexibility to pursue outside interests now that her business is humming along. She invests in early stage companies through her membership with Keiretsu Forum, a worldwide angel organization.

"There are many challenges for women entrepreneurs," she says. "They don't get the same funding that men receive – so this allows me to create a fund that invests in women entrepreneurs. It has allowed me to pursue my passion and has given me financial resources and time to do that."

ERA specialists compete with no one

And the absolute best part of being an ERA franchisee? The field is wide open for ERA franchisees to pursue unlimited opportunities. Small to mid-size businesses pursuing cost-saving reduction projects don't have the width, depth and tenure of ERA.

"We have world-class expense category specialists, franchisees who built their careers in an expense category area, and they do what no procurement team can do," says Michael Nicholas. "Procurement teams are often generalists who do not have the same insider knowledge that our specialists have, and that's what brings significant savings to clients – it's part of our 'secret sauce.'"

Accolades for ERA keep rolling in. ERA is a globally recognized franchise and has earned many awards throughout the years, including:

- Top 200 Franchise Systems Award
- HSBC Franchisor of the Year finalist (British Franchise Association)
- Entrepreneur Magazine's Franchise 500
- Top 100 Global Franchises
- Franchise Research Institution: World-Class Franchise®

ERA has been named a World-Class Franchise® by The Franchise Research Institution 3 years in a row. Franchise companies with this certification have an empirically proven commitment to their franchisees' success. They must have franchisees that are energetic, engaged, profitable, and enthusiastic about the future of their franchise business. According to the research, ERA has a high percentage in all categories, including overall quality, franchisee success, joint success, senior management communication, and local competition.

Still interested in becoming an ERA franchisee?

The license fee is $59,900 in the U.S. There is a 15 percent management service fee (royalty) and a 3 percent marketing fund.

For qualified applicants, your next step is to contact ERA (www.findextraprofit.com) to speak with a franchise consultant, be introduced to your coach/mentor, discuss the opportunity with current franchisees, and continue your discovery process.

ARE FRANCHISEES RISK TAKERS?

WHEN I INTERVIEWED franchisees for the book, *Franchising: The Inside Story,* I asked them how they felt about taking risks. At the time, I thought franchisees were entrepreneurs and that entrepreneurs were risk takers.

And then I got an education!

Franchisees may be (and they may think of themselves as) entrepreneurs, but they do not see themselves as risk takers. That explains why they buy franchises.

Risk takers put everything on the line with little or no assurance of a safety net. When they buy or develop a business they invest their life savings and more (money borrowed from banks, a 401(k) account, or family and friends). For the risk taker, it's do or die.

"Isn't that what franchisees do, too?" you may be asking.

Not really. First of all, if the franchisee selected a franchise company with a good track record, one in which most of the franchisees have succeeded historically, the franchisee's safety net is the franchisor, or the corporate office. The franchisor is responsible for providing the franchisee with a plan for operating the business, plus training and ongoing support. If franchisees have a problem, they contact the franchisor for help, and a good franchisor is responsive and effective.

Franchisees also serve as a safety net for challenged franchisees. A franchisee who can't figure out how to solve a business issue can always contact other franchisees within the network. "What did you do when you were faced with this problem?" Since franchisees of the same brand, i.e. Expense Reduction Analysts, do not compete with each other, they willingly help each other.

Risk takers do not get the advantage of a safety net. It may be that they don't want one – the thrill is not in buying or building the business, but in the risk. When risk takers encounter problems, they don't think about calling a friend in the same business because they are competitors. Instead, risk takers try to figure it out on their own, and that often leads to failure.

Of course, there's still some risk in franchising. "I am a calculated risk taker," one prominent franchisee told me. "You can't be in business without taking some risks, it's the nature of business ownership. However, you don't have to be stupid about it. Or throw caution to the wind. You've got to realize that there's a downside to any business opportunity. So you invest cautiously. You do your homework, and franchising gives you that opportunity. You look around the corner, you think through the pros and cons, and you spend time talking to others who already own a franchise. So, no, I'm not a risk taker. But I take calculated risks as a franchisee."

Makes sense to me. How about you?

17 STEPS TO SUCCESSFULLY BUYING A FRANCHISE

EVERYTHING IS POSSIBLE with a system!

Outstanding achievements are the results of someone following a system. With the right systems you can succeed at almost anything. What is it that you want? There's a system to help you get it.

You want to successfully buy a franchise? It won't surprise you, I don't think, to discover that there's a system for doing so. And here it is: *17 Steps to Successfully Buying a Franchise.* If you follow these guidelines, you're taking all the right steps to explore franchising, to consider the pros and cons of franchising, and, if franchising makes sense for you, to ultimately find a franchise opportunity worthy of your investment.

Even though I cannot guarantee your success as a franchisee – no one can because there are so many variables at play – if you complete these 17 steps you can eventually sign your name to a franchise agreement with the confidence that you've done everything possible to ensure your own success as a franchisee. Of course, you must follow the system and complete each step with integrity.

Based on that understanding, here are 17 steps to successfully buying a franchise:

1. Educate Yourself

As you prepare to buy a franchise, spend time reading (or viewing informational videos) to make sure you understand what franchising is all about. You can also get good information at franchise conferences and through franchise advisors. One way or another, familiarize yourself with the fundamentals of franchising.

> Questions you should ask:
> - *Why is franchising so successful?*
> - *What are the main reasons for franchise failure?*
> - *How can I be sure that a franchisor is legitimate?*

2. Why Franchising Exists

Of all the points that you need to understand about franchising, the most important may be this: *Franchising is a system of distribution.* Franchising is a means for marketing and selling products and services. Don't get caught up in any of the hype about franchising. Yes, of course it's a way for you to own your own business, and it may be the safest way to do so, and it may be your ticket to financial independence, but do not overlook the fundamental purpose of franchising: *It's to sell stuff!*

Questions you should ask:
- *Am I excited about distributing the franchisor's products and services?*
- *Do I see myself operating this system for 10, or more years?*
- *How can I be sure that the franchisor's system will work in my territory?*

3. Does Franchising Make Sense for You?

Be absolutely sure that franchising makes sense for you. Franchisors are not interested in selling franchises to the wrong prospects or investors. You should be equally as protective of yourself. Ask the question: *Is franchising for me?* Keep in mind that it's not for everyone. If it's not for you, don't force it.

Utilize the DiSC personality profile (www.howtobuyafranchise.com/DISC) – it's free!

Questions you should ask:
- *What qualifies me to be a franchisee?*
- *Why do I want to be a franchisee?*
- *What type of franchise will make the most sense for me?*

4. Know Your Role as a Franchisee

Understand that the franchisor creates the *system* and the franchisees follow the system. Good franchisors know what needs to be done day-to-day, month-to-month to succeed in the business. And that's what they'll expect you to do. Everything you're required to do is part of the system, so you must be willing to follow it, even if you don't always agree with it. Otherwise the franchisor can take away your franchise. The franchise agreement mandates that you follow the franchisor's system.

Questions you should ask:
- *How can I learn more about the franchisor's system?*
- *What aspects of the system may or may not be of interest to me?*
- *Do existing franchisees endorse the franchisor's system?*

5. You're Buying a License

By legal definition, a franchise is a license. A franchisor licenses a franchisee to operate a specific business in a specific manner at a specific location (or in a specific region) for a specific period of time. The license can be renewed and either party also can terminate it. Be sure you understand those details before you invest.

Furthermore, the franchisor retains ownership of (almost) everything! The franchisor's intellectual property, training materials, marketing methodologies, sales processes, possibly even phone numbers and clients, always remain the property of the franchisor and not the franchisee. These details will be explained in the Franchise Disclosure Document (FDD).

> Questions you should ask:
> - *What are the specific terms of the franchise agreement?*
> - *Do I get a protected territory? (You may not want a protected territory and you do not necessarily need one, depending on the franchise.)*
> - *What if I decide I want to sell the franchise; how do I do that?*

6. The Franchise Work Environment

Think about the franchise work environment. Most franchisors require franchisees to be owners/operators. In other words, you can't be an absentee owner. Some franchisors expect franchisees to work from home or a small office. Other franchisors require franchisees to work from a retail shop at a strip center or a mall. Other franchisors require franchisees to work from a van or another type of vehicle. In some cases franchisees work alone; in other cases franchisees manage employees. Once you know which work environment makes sense for you, pursue franchise opportunities that support your preferences.

Questions you should ask:
- *Do I want to manage people?*
- *Am I comfortable working alone, from my home or a small office?*
- *If I prefer one work environment but the franchise companies of my choice require a different work environment, can I adjust?*

7. Did You Know They Franchised THAT?

There are at least 75 primary industries that use franchising as their method of distribution. Once people explore franchises, they're surprised by the industries that have developed franchise opportunities It's best to find the industry that makes sense for you. Keep in mind that from industry to industry, franchise investment costs vary.

Questions you should ask:
- *Which industries interest me the most?*
- *Which industries can I afford?*
- *Which industries provide me with the best opportunities?*

8. Look for the Right Opportunity

No one knows how many franchise opportunities exist, but estimates suggest there are 3,000 to 4,000 opportunities in North America alone. Many of these opportunities are local or regional, and some of the companies are sold out so they're not offering franchises except internationally. Some industries include a dozen or more franchise companies offering similar and competitive franchise opportunities, while other industries may only include a handful of franchisors. Of course, these numbers are of little consequence considering that you're looking for just one franchise – the one that's best for you. You will find these opportunities by reading books and articles, attending expos, and by being observant: What's being franchised today that interests you?

Questions you should ask:
- *How much money can I invest in a franchise? The answer may dictate the industries that you should explore.*
- *How do I want to spend the next five, 10, or more years of my life in business?*
- *When it comes to "selling stuff," what excites me?*

9. Information is Free; Ask for It!

When you find a company that interests you, ask for information. It's free, and it comes without any strings attached. Remember, a U.S.-based franchisor must provide U.S. citizens with a disclosure document at least two weeks before selling a franchise. The clock doesn't begin to tick until you acknowledge receiving the disclosure document. And franchisors will not send you that document until they've had an opportunity to speak with you and know that you are qualified to invest in their business.

There's no reason not to ask for information, provided you're genuinely interested in the franchise. You can expect the company to ask you for your personal information before sharing information with you.

Generally, a franchisor wants to get your email address, your phone number, the timeframe in which you plan to buy a franchise, and an understanding of how much money you intend to invest in a business. By the way, it's a mistake to provide misleading information – once you're found out, do you think the franchisor will trust you?

Questions you should ask:
- *Are you planning to open franchises in my territory of choice?*
- *How much is the investment in your franchise?*
- *What makes your franchise business unique and amazing?*

10. Read the Information Carefully

Invest time to carefully read the information provided by the franchisor. Make sure you not only can see yourself as a franchisee, but that you understand the business and the requirements of franchisees in your company of choice. The franchisor's preliminary information may not be specific, but the information in the franchisor's disclosure document must be specific. If you like what you're reading (perhaps even seeing, if the franchisor provides links to videos) plan to ask for the disclosure document.

Questions you should ask:
- *If I were to invest in this franchise, what else would I need to know?*
- *Is this a business that makes sense for my location, or territory?*
- *Where's this business headed in the next five to 10 years?*

11. Attend the Franchisor's Discovery Day

Visit the franchisor. Almost every franchisor sponsors a Discovery Day. This is your chance to visit the franchisor's headquarters, meet company representatives (possibly even franchisees), and learn more about the franchise opportunity by listening to a variety of presentations and asking questions.

The franchisor may also include a tour to show you the training center, the marketing department, etc. Franchisors do not charge a fee for Discovery Days, but you most likely will be expected to provide your own transportation and lodging.

However, don't be afraid to ask the franchisor to pay for your expenses, or to share your expenses – if you decide to join. But even if you have to shell out some money for this experience, it's worth it. If you're married, the franchisor may want your spouse to attend, too.

Questions you should ask:
- *How is this business unique and amazing?*
- *How does this business compare to similar franchises?*
- *What's the future for this industry, and this franchise in particular?*

12. Get Disclosed

Ask the franchisor for the Franchise Disclosure Document (FDD). Once the franchisor knows that you're a "serious" candidate to buy a franchise, by law the franchisor must "disclose" you before continuing to talk to you about the franchise opportunity. This is a very serious matter and franchisors are careful not to violate it.

When you ask for the disclosure document the franchisor will ask you for detailed information to qualify your candidacy. Be prepared to tell the franchisor about your net worth, your personal and professional background (including any criminal violations), and the timeframe in which you plan to buy a franchise. Expect the franchisor to investigate this information by running a credit history and a criminal background check. The franchisor may also require you to complete a franchise personality assessment.

Receiving a FDD does not obligate you to do anything! You must have this document for at least 14 days (not including the day you receive it, nor the 14th day) prior to buying the franchise. But you're not obligated until you sign the franchise agreement.

Questions you should ask:
- *How long has this franchise been in business; who owns it; how are the franchise company's executives qualified to be in their positions?*
- *How much training and support will I receive? Does it cost extra money?*
- *How often (if ever) have franchisees sued the franchisor, and why?*

13. Go to Work for a Franchisee

One of the most important steps you can take before buying a franchise is to talk to existing franchisees. Call them, visit them, and spend time with them. The FDD includes a list of existing and former franchisees – use that list; it's one of the most important tools for franchise exploration.

Existing franchisees will talk to you by phone, or if they're in close proximity to you, they may invite you for a personal meeting. Some franchisees may not be willing to talk to you at all, but most franchisees remember what it was like when they were exploring franchise opportunities, and they're willing to help you because someone once helped them. Franchisees also realize that it's important for their franchise networks to expand – it gives them greater visibility in the marketplace (more franchisees means more money in the national advertising fund) and greater clout when negotiating with suppliers.

Here's an idea that you will find extremely helpful: Go to work for an existing franchisee. Offer to work weekends or part time for a month or more to experience the franchise operation. This is a practical way for you to discover your interest in a specific business. Many franchisors will require that you at least meet with an area developer or an existing franchisee to discuss your prospects for joining the franchise network.

"Are franchisees getting paid to tell me good things so that I'll buy the franchise?" If they are, the information will be revealed in the FDD, or the franchisor is violating federal laws in the U.S.! Generally, franchisors do not pay franchisees for speaking to prospective franchisees. However, franchisors sometimes sponsor competitions (i.e. the franchisee who helps sell the most franchises in a year receives $10,000!). But that information also must be disclosed in the FDD.

Questions you should ask:
- *Would you buy this same franchise again?*
- *What are the franchisor's greatest strengths ... weaknesses?*

14. Decide if You Can Afford the Investment

Study Item 7 of the franchisor's FDD to understand your financial commitment when you buy this franchise. Federal law requires U.S. franchisors to clearly disclose financial information in the FDD. Item 7, Estimated Initial Investment, presents each financial commitment in a chart that shows you when the money is due to be paid, to whom it must be paid (i.e. the franchisor, a media company, a landlord, or a supplier), and whether or not the money is refundable. This is the best way to see the required financial commitment at a glance.

Keep in mind that the franchisor must include every financial requirement in Item 7, which eliminates surprises. "Oh, we didn't tell you that you owe $5,000 for training?" That sort of thing doesn't happen anymore in franchising.

Questions you should ask:
- *Can I afford to invest this amount of money?*
- *Do existing franchisees say that the investment is reasonable?*
- *How does this financial commitment compare to investments in competitive opportunities?*

15. Understand the Ongoing Fees

Look at the ongoing royalty and advertising fee requirements, which are not part of Item 7. Most franchisors require franchisees to pay a percentage of gross sales as a royalty every month – the percentage may be as low as 5 percent and as high as 15 percent, and varies from company to company. The advertising fee is also a percentage of gross sales and may be in the range of 1 percent to 3 percent.

Questions you should ask:
- *Do the royalty and advertising fees seem reasonable?*
- *How does the franchisor spend the royalty dollars paid by franchisees?*
- *Is the national advertising fund effective for boosting retail sales?*

16. Get Help!

Consult with your professional advisors. You should spend the money to engage a franchise attorney and an accountant prior to signing a franchise agreement. There are many franchise attorneys at work in the U.S. and other countries. You can find them through a franchise association such as the International Franchise Association at Franchise.org. You will likely pay $500 to $1,500 for the attorney's basic services. You will likely pay more money to an attorney who does not specialize in franchise law – that's like asking your franchise attorney to handle a personal injury suit. If an attorney suggests he/she negotiate with the franchisor on your behalf, be very careful. Franchisors rarely negotiate and franchise attorneys know that. However, franchise attorneys also know areas in which a franchisor is likely to negotiate and may be helpful in that regard.

It's more difficult to find an accountant who is familiar with franchising and who understands franchising. Too often accountants are anti-franchising and they advise their clients to start businesses independently rather than to join a franchise network and pay fees. That's unfortunate because statistics demonstrate that in many industries franchises are more successful than independently owned businesses. My best advice for finding a "franchise friendly" accountant is to find an accountant who is also a franchisee! In other words, the accountant's practice is part of a franchise network. You can find these businesses through franchise associations. A good accountant will be able to help you develop a business plan and assess your financial risk as well as rewards. Accounting fees vary widely, but for basic services expect to pay $500 to $1,500. Keep in mind that you also may need an accountant after you become a franchisee to prepare your quarterly and annual statements.

Keep in mind that professional advisors are not supposed to make decisions for you. "Should I buy this franchise?" is a question that a good advisor will not answer. Advisors will point out pros and cons; ultimately, you make the decisions.

Other possible advisors include franchise brokers and coaches. When you engage these advisors, make certain that you understand what's in it for them. Brokers sell franchises for a living; they do not advise franchise prospects except as part of their mission to sell a franchise. Brokers generally do not charge fees to their clients because the franchisor pays them when they sell a franchise. There's nothing wrong with this arrangement, by the way, and franchisors who rely on brokers must reveal this information in the FDD.

Questions you should ask:
- *How does this franchise opportunity compare to others you've reviewed?*
- *What are the problem areas that you see investing in this type of franchise?*
- *Based on my financial situation, is this a franchise I can afford?*

17. Make Your Final Decision

Take a deep breath, offer up any final prayers, and say yes to the franchisor of your choice. Go ahead; sign the franchise agreement. Congratulations, you're a franchisee! If you did your homework, and followed the recommendations offered to you in this book and through other sources, you're on your way to your new business venture!

Questions you should as
- *When does my training session begin?*
- *What three things must I be sure to do to succeed in this business?*

- *What three things must I be sure* not *to do to succeed in this business?*

When I'm buying a franchise, and when I coach my clients who are buying franchises, I use these 17 steps to success. Each step includes multiple tasks, and it's important to take the time to complete each step. If you have questions about how to complete these steps, or you need additional guidance, visit my blog at HowToBuyAFranchise.com and contact me.

FUNDING YOUR FRANCHISE ACQUISITION: WHERE DO YOU GET THE MONEY?

TWO COMMON MISTAKES that prospective franchisees make when they're exploring franchise opportunities are: (1) ignorance of their personal financial status and capabilities and (2) ignorance of the financial requirements to buy a franchise.

Do you know your credit score and how much cash you can invest in a franchise or bring to the table to leverage additional funds? Do you know what banks, leasing companies, the U.S Small Business Administration, and special funds designated for franchise lending will require of you to secure a loan?

The sooner you get on top of these issues the better – otherwise, you may be wasting your time. You should expect franchisors and franchise brokers to ask you these questions even before they give you a Franchise Disclosure Document. Not to do so could mean the franchisor is wasting time because you may not be financially qualified to acquire the franchise.

Good News for Borrowers

If you need to borrow money to acquire a franchise, the good news is that for the first time in many years you have multiple options available. While it was nearly impossible to borrow money to start a franchise between 2008 and 2010, opportunities are more plentiful today but still not what they were before the Great Recession.

While there's still not a national lender for franchise opportunities as existed prior to 2008, nowadays more community banks lend to franchisees, and for those who have a retirement fund, the fund can be rolled into seed money to capitalize a business.

"Compared to what it was like before the recession, funding franchises is still difficult," explains Bob Coleman, editor of the Coleman Report, which provides information to bankers to help them make less risky small-business loans.

"Lenders are scrutinizing deals and are particularly interested in the performance of the brand, something that didn't matter as much previously."

Not Good News for New Brands

"Unless a franchisor has 80 to 100 units, there's no deal," continues Coleman. "A startup brand and a new franchisee is not a favorable combination. Lenders want to see track records from both the brand and the franchisee. Lenders today know about unhappy franchisees and how to check for them, whereas (previously) they didn't care – [pay] 30 percent [money] down and you'd get the loan, but that doesn't happen anymore."

According to Coleman, lenders view franchises as "a little bit better risk than mom-and-pop businesses," but they're insisting on funding deals for established brands. They also prefer experienced franchisees. "If you've been successfully operating a unit for several years and now you need money to open another one to three units, you can get that money."

How Do You Get a Loan Today?

So what's it going to take today to get the money you need to acquire a franchise opportunity?

Business financing expert Doug Smith of Biz Finance Solutions in Colorado, explains that there are two types of funding: equity-based and debt-based.

"Using the money you have in your retirement plan, rolling it over without penalty or taxation, and using it as an injection to get a U.S. government-backed loan is equity financing," he says, and it's an option that many franchisees use today.

"Debt based funding requires a credit score and credit history to get a conventional bank loan or unsecured business financing, including equipment leasing, and unsecured personal loans. But if your credit score is weak or you've filed a bankruptcy, it's the kiss of death."

Your personal financial situation, and your thoughts about financial risk, may determine how you should proceed when you seek financing.

The 401(k) Rollover

Smith's preferred franchise funding strategy is the 401(k) Rollover, and most people don't seem to know about it. Or if they do, they've been told it's illegal or dangerous. However, this option has the blessing of the U.S. government. Here are the facts you need to know:

If you have a retirement fund and you change employers, you have three important options:
1. Leave the fund where it is. The majority of people choose this option.

2. Move the fund into a new account, such as a self-directed IRA.
3. Move the fund to your new employer's 401(k), thus consolidating your retirement savings in one fund.

Most people aren't aware of Option #3, beginning with becoming your own employer!

That is, you can become a franchisee and establish a C Corporation with stock and a 401(k). Becoming your own employer puts you in the enviable position of self-funding your own business, tax-free! You can move – or what the Internal Revenue Service refers to as rollover – your existing retirement money into your new employer's 401k, and the cash can be used to buy and operate a franchise. It's tax-free, penalty-free (if done correctly), and it's legal. It may be your best option for funding your business, particularly if you don't have other resources, or you can't qualify for a traditional loan.

Isn't This Controversial?

The U.S. Internal Revenue Service and the Department of Labor have established guidelines and directives for implementing a 401(k) Rollover. You can't use the rollover to dodge taxes or to personally benefit from the money. Some years ago a financial broker was shut down for a period of time for stretching the rules, and that incident gave rise to the notion that the rollover is illegal. It's not. If you use the rollover for the right reasons – you can't use it for a scheme; it has to be used with a real business – you (or your advisor) set it up correctly and comply annually with the regulations, you should be able to avoid any objections or complications. Follow the spirit of the guidelines with appropriate intentions and you should remain in the clear.

Of course, the IRS reserves the right to change the rules, and that's why it's extremely important that you work with a credible company or broker that has a track record for successfully implementing and maintaining rollovers.

Two Benefits of a 401(k) Rollover

The 401(k) Rollover has made a good name for itself among franchisors, who frequently recommend the strategy to prospective franchisees.

Here are two reasons why:

- If the franchise acquisition is a small investment – under $150,000 – franchisors know that lenders aren't attracted to small loans. There's no money to be made processing small loans, so lenders avoid them. That makes a rollover more attractive. Rollover money can be used to pay for the franchise fee and to buy equipment. When you don't have collateral – or you're buying a business that provides a service from your home, a vehicle, or a small office – the 401(k) Rollover may be your best choice for funding your business.

- After a rollover, you can use the cash as equity to qualify for a conventional or SBA-guaranteed loan. You'll likely need a cash injection of 30 percent to secure a loan. In the past, borrowers used equity in real estate (i.e. their personal residence) to qualify for a loan. Now you can use rollover money for your cash injection.

"People who utilize a rollover are more successful in the average business," reveals Geoff Seiber, president and CEO of FranFund.com in Fort Worth, Texas. "People who use this strategy tend to stay in business longer because they used their retirement money to fund their business and they don't have debt to service."

Can You Accept the Risks?

Used properly, the 401(k) Rollover is an aggressive way to capitalize your business. The challenge, however, is that by using it you give up the security of a retirement fund. Some people can't handle that emotionally. *Can you?* Will you feel comfortable knowing that your retirement money is now invested in your own business? If not, you probably don't want to use this funding strategy. On the other hand, people who start businesses and plan to operate them aren't usually looking for comfort.

In the U.S., numerous companies provide rollover services, including: Biz Finance Solutions, Guidant, FranFund, and Benetrends. Expect to spend about $5,000 with one of these firms to set up your rollover. The firm will also offer to provide necessary administrative services to keep your fund in check, and that may cost you about $100 monthly.

It's important to keep your rollover plan in compliance with the laws because the IRS audits these plans. "Under 2 percent of our plans are audited every year," says Seiber, "which is the norm in our industry. By not doing the administrative work properly, you're taking a bigger risk" if the IRS audits your account.

Options to the 401(k) Rollover

Unless you have a pile of cash that you intend to inject into your deal (i.e. a retirement fund that you will rollover or savings that you will bring to the table), your funding options are severely limited. It's even worse if you're a new franchisee and you want to buy a single unit – an existing franchisee with plans to expand or a multi-unit operator will find more options.

Look to Your Franchisor for Funding

Guys like Coleman, Smith, and Seiber are among a select corps of experts who can advise prospective franchisees when they need financing, but there's only so much they can do in a reticent financial market. If you can't take advantage of the programs they offer or recommend, so ask your finance-related questions early in your franchise exploration.

And don't give up! Some of the most successful franchisees today started out by investing in a low-cost franchise and expanding when they could afford to do so. Many others started out with money borrowed from family and friends. If franchising makes sense for you, you'll find a franchise company that can offer suggestions.

HERE'S AN INCENTIVE FOR QUALIFIED VETERANS: VETFRAN

VETFRAN.COM SPONSORED by the International Franchise Association (IFA, www.franchise.org) helps veterans of the U.S. armed services buy franchise opportunities by providing financial assistance, training, and industry support.

VetFran was created by the late Don Dwyer Sr., founder of The Dwyer Group, a conglomerate of franchise companies, to say "thank you" to America's veterans returning from the first Gulf War. After the Sept. 11, 2001 terrorist attacks, IFA re-launched VetFran and the program continues to this day.

Nearly 650 franchise brands voluntarily offer financial incentives and mentoring to prospective franchisees who are veterans. Thousands of veterans have utilized VetFran to buy franchises. If you're a veteran, be sure to ask your franchisor of choice, "Do you support VetFran?" This may be an additional source of funding for you. Ask the franchisor if he participates in this incentive, as some franchisors that do, will also allow for a discount on their initial franchise fee.

Foreign Investors: Use Franchising to Get a U.S. Green Card

Foreign investors who want to move to the USA are taking advantage of the Immigrant Investor Program administered by the U.S. Citizenship and Immigration Services (USCIS). Applications are rising rapidly due to favorable changes in the program, and in part due to franchising.

Known as EB-5, the program was created to stimulate the U.S. economy through job creation and capital investment.

Here's how it works:

How the EB5 program works

A qualified foreigner invests $1-million directly into a business or into a regional fund that invests in businesses, including franchises of all types. If the investment creates at least 10 full-time jobs for at least two years, the investor gets a green card and eventually U.S. citizenship. In high unemployment areas, and rural areas, the investment is $500,000.

Foreign investors are using EB-5 to move their families to the U.S. or to send their children to the U.S. to study. A married investor gets visas for himself, his spouse, and all unmarried children under the age of 21.

Franchisors favor foreign operators

Foreigners operate many franchised businesses in the U.S. and franchisors welcome them because they are enthusiastic about learning a successful operating system that they and their family members can operate. However, EB-5 does not require investors to actually work in a business. As long as they fulfill the requirements of EB-5, the investors can live wherever they choose, start their own business, take a job, or retire in the U.S.!

As with any bureaucratic program, EB-5 takes time to complete. Investors must prove their money came from a lawful source and must also pass the scrutiny of U.S. immigration investors. The entire process may require a year before the investor and family can move to the U.S.

Direct and in-direct jobs count

Until recently, most EB-5 investors preferred real estate projects, but many of those investments failed to meet the job requirements. Franchising, on the other hand, is a much better choice. An injection of $1-million invested into certain franchised businesses can create upwards of 40 jobs. Consider, for example, a convenience store franchise. The franchise itself may need only

4 to 6 employees, but indirect jobs also count. A convenience store sells food and beverages and indirectly creates jobs to provide those products. Those indirect jobs count.

Franchisors are unaware of EB-5

Many franchise networks include multi-unit operators who seek expansion capital, and sometimes partners, to open a dozen or more units, or to expand into a new territory. However, most franchisors don't know this program exists, so their multi-unit operators may not know, either.

USCIS.gov is a good place to learn more about this program.

Franchise Terms and Resources

THE FOLLOWING LISTS provide information about franchising, including resources that may help you while you're pursuing a franchise opportunity. Please keep in mind that the inclusion of any resource does not imply the author's endorsement. The information in these lists is not exhaustive. If you're looking for something that you can't find in this section, please visit HowToBuyAFranchise.com and use our Contact form.

Franchise Terms

Here are some of the most common terms used in franchising.

Advertising Fee

Many franchise opportunities require franchisees to pay a monthly fee into an Advertising or Marketing Fund. The fee is generally represented as a percentage (for example, 3 percent) and is almost always calculated on the franchisee's gross sales, as opposed to net sales or profits. The Advertising Fee may also be a flat fee. The Advertising Fee is ongoing and will be collected while the franchise agreement is in effect. Advertising Fund monies are used to advertise the franchise brand, its products and/or services. This is not money to be used by the franchisor!

Ad Fund

Franchisees pay their Advertising Fees into an Ad Fund, which is used to underwrite the cost of advertising and promotions for franchisees. The franchisor, or Franchise Advisory Council, establishes the Ad Fund and oversees it on behalf of franchisees. Ad Fund money is often used to hire advertising and marketing agencies to assist the franchise network.

Disclosure

In some countries, and especially in the United States, franchisors are *required* by federal and some state laws to "disclose" individuals who are serious about acquiring a franchise. Disclosure is a process that includes providing prospective franchisees with a copy of the franchisor's Franchise Disclosure Document (FDD) and

Franchise Agreement. The FDD must be delivered to a franchise candidate at least 10 days – not including the day you receive it, nor the 10th day – prior to the candidate purchasing the franchise. Disclosure minimizes fraudulent sales in franchising and promotes the safety and longevity of franchising. Franchisors are required to comply with specific disclosure regulations that disseminate helpful information to prospective franchisees in advance of paying any money or signing any documents.

Disclosure Document
See Franchise Disclosure Document.

Earning's Claim
An Earning's Claim (or a Financial Performance Representation), often known as Item 19 may be included in a franchisor's Franchise Disclosure Document. An Earning's Claim documents the earnings of franchisees in the franchisor's network.

Most franchisors do not include Earning's Claims in their documents. Those who do not are prohibited from making any oral or written statements concerning the actual or potential sales, costs, income or profits of their franchise opportunities.

Franchise
It's a license that grants an individual or an entity (i.e. a corporation) the right to use a franchisor's operating system for the purpose of

marketing, selling and distributing the franchisor's products and/or services. A franchise is a license.

Franchise Agreement

A legal document (license) signed by both the franchisor and the franchisee granting the franchisee the right to operate the franchise system for a specified period of time, in a specified format, and sometimes in a specified location. It's the legally binding document between franchisor and franchisee.

Franchise Associations

There are approximately 40 trade associations throughout the world that represent the interests of franchisors and franchisees. See International Franchise Association.

Franchise Disclosure Document

Every franchisor in the U.S. is required to complete and maintain a Franchise Disclosure Document (FDD). The FDD, in layperson's language, describes the franchise opportunity. The items of disclosure are standard for all franchise companies. There are 23 Items that require disclosure, including Litigation, Initial Franchise Fee, Franchisee's Obligations, Franchisor's Obligations, Territory, Restrictions On What The Franchisee May Sell, Renewal, Termination, Transfer and Dispute Resolution, List of Outlets (Franchisees), Financial Statements, and more.

Prospective franchisees should read the FDD several times before investing in the franchise.

Franchisee
The individual or entity (i.e. a corporation) that's assigned the rights to a franchise by a franchisor.

Franchise Expo
Franchise companies come together under one roof to exhibit their franchise opportunities for a day or more. The public is invited to these events. Expos sometimes include educational programs.

Franchise Fee
A one-time, upfront fee required by the franchisor. It must be disclosed in the Franchise Disclosure Document.

Franchise Portal
A website that promotes franchise opportunities and may also include educational information about franchising. Good examples: FranchiseExpo.com, FranchiseHelp.com.

Franchisor
The company that grants franchises to franchisees. The franchisor controls and owns the franchise system.

International Franchise Association

IFA (www.franchise.org) is the world's largest trade organization representing both franchisors and franchisees. Headquarters: Washington, D.C.

International Franchise Expo

A world premier event sponsored by the International Franchise Association. The producer of the IFE (www.ifeinfo.com) is MFVExpositions.

Royalty Fee

A payment of money by the franchisee to the franchisor. Usually represented as a percentage Royalties are almost always paid on the franchisee's gross sales, as opposed to net sales or profits. This is an ongoing fee that must be paid during the period of time the franchise agreement/license is in effect. The royalty fee must be disclosed in the Franchise Disclosure Document.

FRANCHISE RESOURCES

Franchise Associations

International Franchise Association
1900 K St., NW, Suite 700
Washington, DC 20006
Phone: (202) 628-8000
www.franchise.org

In addition to representing franchisors and franchisees, the IFA also represents the Council of Franchise Suppliers, which includes attorneys, accountants, consultants, franchise brokers, and others who may be able to assist you in your exploration of franchising. IFA promotes numerous books and other resources about franchising and publishes *Franchising World* magazine. Free resources are included on the IFA's website.

Canadian Franchise Association
5399 Eglinton Ave. West, Suite 116
Toronto, Ontario
Canada M9C 5K6
Telephone: 416-695-2896
Email: info@cfa.ca

For a list of Franchise Associations Worldwide:
www.franchise.org

Franchise Expositions

MFV Expositions
Telephone: 201-226-1130

In addition to the International Franchise Expo, MFV Expositions produces the West Coast Franchise Expo, Franchise Expo South and international franchise events including *Feria Internacional de Franquicias* in Mexico City.

U.S. Government Resources

U.S. Small Business Administration
U.S. Commerce Department International Trade Administration

Books, Periodicals & Portals

7 Dirty Little Secrets of Franchising: Protect Your Franchise Investment, Amazon.com
12 Amazing Franchise Opportunities for 2015, Amazon.com
101 Questions to Ask Before You Invest in a Franchise, Amazon.com
Bond's Franchise Guide, Amazon.com
Buy "Hot" Franchises Without Getting Burned, Amazon.com
Entrepreneur publishes the Franchise 500 every January
Franchise Handbook
FranchiseExpo.com
FranchiseGator.com

Making Money While Saving Money

Franchise Opportunities Guide
Franchise Times
Franchise Update
Franchising World

AUTHOR'S BIOGRAPHY

John P. Hayes, Ph.D., began working in the franchise community in 1979 as a freelance writer. He continues to write about franchising for media worldwide, including newspapers, magazines and books.

On several occasions he has been a franchisee, and for several years he served as the President & CEO of one of America's major franchise companies, HomeVestors of America, Inc. He is one of the few people to have been a franchisee, a franchisor, and an advisor to franchisors and franchisees.

In 2017, Dr. Hayes was appointed the Titus Chair for Franchise Leadership and director of the Titus Center for Franchising (www.pba.edu/titus-center) at Palm Beach Atlantic University in West Palm Beach, Florida.

For many years Dr. Hayes' client list included the International Franchise Association (IFA), the International Franchise Expo (IFE), and dozens of franchise companies. For several years he toured the USA as part of IFA's regional training faculty, and on many occasions he has been a speaker and trainer for IFA, the IFE, and countless franchise companies. For several years starting in 1989, he traveled with the IFA's international franchise trade missions, marketing U.S. franchise opportunities in Europe, South America, the Pacific Rim, and the Far East.

Dr. Hayes is a frequent speaker at international franchise expos, and a guest on radio and television to discuss franchise topics. He was featured in a 30-minute television infomercial called *The Power of Franchising*. Through the years he has assisted franchisors and franchisees internationally to sell or acquire master licensing rights. For nearly 30 years he has taught the most popular symposium at the International Franchise Expo: The A to Zs of Buying a Franchise.

He is the author or co-author of more than 25 non-fiction books. His bestsellers include **Take the Fear Out of Franchising**, **Buy "Hot" Franchises Without Getting Burned**, and **101 Questions to Ask Before You Invest in a Franchise**. He is the co-author of **Franchising: The Inside Story** (with John Kinch); **You Can't Teach a Kid to Ride a Bike at a Seminar** (with David Sandler); **Start Small, Finish Big**, *15 Lessons to Start & Operate Your Own Business*, (with the co-founder of Subway); and **Network Marketing for Dummies** (with Zig Ziglar). His books are listed at BooksByJohnHayes.com.

He was formerly a professor at Gulf University for Science & Technology (Kuwait), Temple University and Kent State University.

BizComPress

Do you have a story to tell that will help others improve their life, their business, or otherwise make a difference? BizComPress can help you reach the widest audience possible. Founded by authors for authors, BizComPress is a new kind of publishing company. Our award-winning team will help you write your book, edit it, design it, publish it, and promote it. And you keep the majority of your earnings!

Whether you already have a manuscript, or just the seed of an idea, contact us and we'll provide honest feedback based on decades of experience in book publishing. If we think the manuscript or the idea has a market, we can develop a plan that fits your budget. You'll be on your way to becoming a published author.

For more information contact Scott White at BizComPress.com or via phone: 214-458-5751.

Contact
Expense Reduction Analysts

US Headquarters:
Addison Tower
16415 Addison Rd., Suite 410
Addison, TX 75001

Telephone:
877.299.7801

Website:
www.expensereduction.com

ONE LAST THING

Now that you've read *Making Money While Saving Money please visit Amazon.com and take just a few moments to post a review on the book's sales page at* http://www.amazon.com/dp/B073RW9KD1. We'll be grateful for your honest review. It can be brief, or as detailed as you prefer.

Thank you.